"The Little Book of Criminal Investigations"

Larry D. Anthony, Ph. D.

RoseDog Books
PITTSBURGH, PENNSYLVANIA 15238

RoseDog Books
585 Alpha Drive, Suite 103
Pittsburgh, PA 15238
Visit our website at *www.rosedogbookstore.com*

ISBN: 979-8-88729-185-7
eISBN: 979-8-88729-685-2

About the Author

Larry D. Anthony is an Assistant Professor in the Helms School of Government for Liberty University. He holds a Bachelor of Science in Organizational Management from Tusculum University, a Master's in Criminal Justice from Boston University, and a Ph. D. from Walden University. He is a veteran of the U.S. Air Force and U.S. Marine Corps. Dr. Anthony's dissertation, *Police culture and decision making"* has been downloaded worldwide over 5,600 times. He developed and instructed P.O.S.T. Certified courses in Crime Scene Management, Basic Criminal Investigations, Intelligence Collections Methods, Gangs/Terrorists, and other law enforcement subjects presented to Agencies throughout the Midsouth. Dr. Anthony has written on several criminal justice subjects; Police, citizens and oversight: fixing our broken relationship with the public (*Law Enforcement Today*), Law Enforcement Challenges in the 21st Century (*Police Chief Magazine), and Police and the Social Media Battlefield.* He is a retired Memphis Police Captain and Tennessee Bureau of Investigation Intelligence Analyst. He was called to active duty in 2004 and served as an Instructor at the U.S. Air Force Security Forces Academy, San Antonio, TX, Security Forces Superintendent on the Crisis Action Team, Washington, D.C., and 5th Air Expeditionary Security Forces Operations Chief, Kuwait City, Kuwait.

Table of Contents

Chapter 1

The Criminal Investigator

"It often seems to me that's all detective work is, wiping out your false starts and beginning again" (Agatha Christie, 1890-1976).

A uniform patrol officer is promoted and assigned to an investigative bureau under the supervision of a Lieutenant who is highly respected and noted for his investigator abilities. A technique the Lieutenant uses for training novice investigators is using a red pen on arrest reports (case investigations) submitted by the investigators to scrutinize the conduct of the investigation. He questions every aspect of the investigation and returns the report to the Investigator, who then must correct and respond to the Lieutenant's remarks. This technique promotes attention to detail, scrutiny of facts[1], and the development of investigative skills.

A newly promoted investigator worked under this Lieutenant for almost a year and was accustomed to getting his arrest reports returned with numerous red marks. The Investigator did not realize that as he conducted more investigations, the red marks were becoming fewer and more professionally focused. One day the Lieutenant handed back the Investigator's latest arrest report. The Investigator carefully examined every line of the report and, to his amazement, found no red marks. With great concern, the Investigator approached the Lieutenant and asked, "Sir, I don't see any red marks. What is the problem with this report?" The Lieutenant

---

[1] "A fact is information minus emotion. An opinion is information plus experience. Ignorance is an opinion lacking information. And, stupidity is opinion that ignores a fact" (Unknown).

replied, "Nothing. It is a good piece of investigation." The Investigator's chest began to swell, and his head began to puff up, and he thought to himself, "Finally, I am a criminal investigator." But, just then, the Lieutenant said, "You have done a great job with evidence collection and documentation, good interviews, good crime scene coverage, and you have without a doubt proved the suspect is guilty. Now prove to me your suspect didn't do it." The Investigator was exasperated and confused. Finally, he said to the Lieutenant, "Sir, I don't understand. I have evidence and statements that prove this guy did it, and now you want me to prove he didn't?" The Lieutenant replied it might be possible that when you developed the suspect, you subconsciously began to connect the evidence with his guilt and proceeded to prove his guild without considering he may be innocent. This is human nature, but a professional criminal investigator not only looks at the evidence but the validity of the evidence. You achieve two things if you try to prove the suspect did not commit the crime. One, you may have made a mistake, and the suspect is actually innocent, and two, you have closed all the doors a defense attorney could open to exonerate the suspect.

It is human nature to focus on a person as a suspect when collaborating evidence points to that person. The Lieutenant's admonition to prove the suspect did not commit the crime is an exercise in objectivity. If an investigator believes a person to be guilty of a crime they will at times subconsciously manipulate the evidence to prove their suspicion of guilt. The person may have a criminal record, look and act like a thug, and is generally unpleasant, but these things are not proof of guilt. In every investigation there is always one more thing to do, and that thing may be found years later by investigators for a defense attorney. Your investigation is complete if a defense attorney investigator cannot find "that thing" in the future.

Chapter 2

The Investigation Begins

"It is by doubting that we come to investigate, and by investigating that we recognize the truth" (Peter Abelard, 1079-1182)

A criminal investigation begins with observation, information, evidence collection, documentation, training, and experience. At every crime scene, something is left or taken away from the scene. Investigators look for things on the scene that should be there but are not or see things on the scene that should not be there but are. Investigators should stay open-minded and receptive to advice or information from anyone. There are three basic principles to a successful criminal investigation. Suspect everyone, believe nothing and check everything.

Investigators received a call about a homicide in a home in a moderate-income community. Upon arriving, investigators discovered a male victim in a bedroom dressed in his underwear lying on the bed. There was one shot to the right temple of the victim, one shot to his chest, and one round in the wall facing the foot of his bed. There was no weapon. There were no signs of forced entry; all doors and windows were locked and secure. There was no written note indicating a suicide. Crime Scene technicians directed by the investigators conducted a video and still photography documentation of the scene. In the victim's bedroom was a landline phone (cell phones had not come into the market), TV and VCR, a computer, an audio cassette, books, and pictures.

A records check of the victim's phone showed his last call was to his parents and a call a few hours earlier to a male friend. First, investigators went to the parents' home in a medium-income community. The house was well kept, neat, and clean. The parents were middle-aged, educated, employed by local businesses, and were devout Roman Catholics. The parents advised their son appeared to be healthy and happy when they last spoke with him and could not offer suggestions for a possible murder suspect. Investigators next went to the home of the victim's male friend. He advised that he and the victim had been in a homosexual relationship for several months. The friend stated he had been dating another man and broke off the relationship with the victim, who became distraught and angry at the ending of the affair.

Investigators spoke with people in the victim's neighborhood but discovered no helpful information. Police dispatch records were checked for possible prowlers, suspicious vehicles, and reported crimes in the area. No leads. The victim's bank and credit card accounts were checked, but no unusual activity was found. Deliveries to the neighborhood were checked, and drivers were interviewed. No leads. The mailman, garbage man, yard man, and other service personnel were interviewed. No leads. One neighborhood home had video surveillance that was checked. No leads. Investigators had exhausted every possible venue that might provide a lead. No luck. A different set of investigators repeated the entire process. No leads. A meeting was held in a conference room with all the investigators in the squad to review each step of the investigation. Nothing new was found.

Two uniform patrol officers were in the squad room on some other business, and one of the investigators suggested asking the senior officer to look at the crime scene to determine if he could see something that may have been overlooked. The senior officer did not discover anything new. The senior officer was asked about his partner and he stated that the officer was a rookie with only a couple of months on the job. The Investigator decided to give the rookie officer an opportunity to give his opinion in a major investigation. The rookie officer looked over the crime scene pictures for several minutes and then asked about the VCR and was told there was nothing significant in the VCR. The rookie asked about the computer and again was told nothing there. The rookie then asked about the audio cassette. Investigators looked at each other and discovered no one had checked the cassette. The cassette was recovered from the evidence locker, and the entire shooting was on the audio. The victim was heard to say he could not live without his lover and was going to end his despair. He had a gun but wanted to be sure it worked, so he fired a bullet into the wall at the foot of his bed (shot 1). Then he stated he was ready to go and fired a bullet into his chest (shot 2) and began yelling about the pain, and fired another shot into his head (shot 3).

Investigators now believed the victim's death was a suicide and that someone had tampered with the crime scene. A report from the coroner's office confirmed the investigators' suspicions. Blood was on the victim's right hand from the blowback of the inflicted head wound, and the position and contact of the wound indicated a self-inflicted gunshot. A gunshot residue test showed positive on the victim's right hand. The position and contact of the chest wound supported the hypothesis. Additionally, investigators confirmed the victim was right-handed and owned a .38 caliber revolver.

Investigators went to the home of the victim's parents and confronted them with the new evidence. After speaking with the parents for a few minutes, they admitted to taking their son's revolver from the crime scene and hiding it in the attic of their home. The mother was deeply troubled that her son would not be given a church funeral or allowed burial in the church cemetery if his death resulted from suicide[2].

The investigation begins with police communications. A victim or witness calls the police to report an incident, and the police dispatcher then contacts the appropriate responders. An investigator should go to communications and check for all calls around the crime scene, from 30 minutes before the first call to 30 minutes after the call. Keep this record for refer-

---

[2] "From the sixth through the late 20th century, the Church technically did not bury anyone who willfully committed suicide... the Church eventually dropped the ban on funerals for suicides from its law code altogether in the 1980s" (Dine, 2020).

ence as the investigation proceeds. If it is a sex crime or missing child, obtain names from the sexual offender register of offenders living or working from within a one to three mile radius of the scene. Check with the Bureau of Prisons for any former felons living or working in the area. Check the local jail for anyone arrested within 1 mile of the scene and anyone released from jail that lives or works in the area 3 hours before the incident. Check homes and businesses for several blocks around the scene for video. Check uniform police logs from patrols in the area for traffic stops or suspicious persons. The weather at the time of the crime can be a factor. Check with the National Weather Service for conditions at the time of the crime. Temperature and humidity can affect evidence. The National Weather Service should be contacted to obtain information of the weather conditions at the time and location of the incident. Anything that could affect a crime scene should be considered. Sources to check that may provide some possible leads are limited only by the Investigator's imagination.

Chapter 3

Interrogation / Interview

"When the Spirit of truth comes, he will guide you into all the truth, for he will not speak on his own authority, but whatever he hears he will speak, and he will declare to you the things that are to come" (English Standard Version , 2001/2022, John 16:13).

Truth is elusive in a criminal investigation and finding it requires discipline, objectivity, listening, watching, and verifying. Novice investigators are sometimes overwhelmed when tasked with taking statements from victims, witnesses, and suspects. Following is a basic format for taking statements that are informative and within Constitutional protections. Every question in a statement can lead to other questions, but these examples provide the basic necessary information.

Victim's Statement

Statement of (name of victim, sex, race, age, DOB, social security number, driver's license number). Home address (number and apartment/lot number, street, city, state, zip code). Home telephone number, including area code. Occupation (type of work, work hours, days off). Place of employment (name of company, address, street, office number, city, state, zip code). Business telephone number including area code. Email address, FAX number. Education (number of years of school completed, degrees, names of schools).

Next of Kin/Emergency contact (name of person, sex, race, age, dob, SSN, relationship, home address, home phone, work address, work phone.

Statement made in the City Police Department, Room 1010, Criminal Justice Complex, 201 Justice Avenue, Somewhere, Tennessee 3810-1973.
Day, date, time. Statement made to (name of investigators and ID).
Name of persons present (all investigators, attorneys, doctors).
Questioned by: Name of Investigators.
Typed by: Name of typist.
Interview taped or videoed by: name of operator.
This statement is being taken relative to the (type of crime) of (name of victim, sex, race, age) which occurred at (location) on (day, date, time).
Report or Identifier number.

Q: Were you the victim of a (shooting, robbery, rape, kidnapping, etc)?
A:

Q: Where did this event occur? (day, date, time).
A:

Q: Do you know the person responsible?

A:
Q: What is your relationship to the suspect?
A:

Q: Can you identify the suspect if you see him again?
A:

Q: Describe the suspect? (Sex, race, age, height, weight, hair (type/color), eyes, scars, marks, tattoos, appearance (clean, dirty, perfume, body odor, alcohol), build (fat, slender, muscular, skinny), speech impediment, accent, smell of breath, clothing description, mood (angry, emotional, etc.
A:

Q: What did the suspect do when he first encountered you? (This maybe emotional and/or embarrassing to the victim. In sex related and child crimes a female investigator should be available to conduct the victim interview).
A:

Q: Who was present when this incident occurred? (relationship to persons present during the incident)
A:

Q: Was the suspect armed?
A:

Q: Describe the weapon.
A:

Q: What did the suspect do with the weapon after the incident?
A:

Q: Where did the suspect go after the incident?
A:

Q: How did the suspect leave the scene? (in a car, on foot, taxi, etc).
A:

Q: Who left with the suspect?
A:

Q: Describe this person.
A:

Q: Who else was involved in this incident?
A:

Q: Who was present before the incident occurred?
A:

Q: Who was present during the incident?
A:

Q: Who was present after the incident?
A:

Q: Who saw this incident occur?
A:

Q: Who did you contact after the incident? (a statement will be needed from this person).
A:

Q: Were you injured by the suspect? (describe the injuries, make photographs)
A:

Q: Did you receive treatment for your injuries? (Where was the victim treated and by whom. A statement will also be needed from this person, and a copy of the treatment received from the hospital.)
A:

Q: Tell me in your own words how this incident happened.
A:

Q: Is there anything you wish to add to this statement?
A:

Q: Can you read without the aid of eyeglasses?

A:

Signature of the person giving the statement (all originals should be signed in red)

Signature of all witnesses present

Date:______________________ Day:____________________ Time:_____

NOTE:

Have the victim initial the bottom of each page and initial each correction in the statement. This should be done in red ink.

Let the victim elaborate about arguments, fights, or whatever they wish. Develop the full series of events preceding and up to the time the victim was removed from the scene.

If the suspect is not in custody ask the victim if they know where the suspect lives, works, or hangs out. Has the victim been in contact with the suspect since the incident? Who might know the location of the suspect?

If a weapon has been recovered, have the victim identify the weapon if possible. This is only a guideline, attempt to obtain as much information as possible that may lead to other witnesses, suspects, evidence, scenes, or other information.

Witness Statement

Statement of (name of witness, sex, race, age, DOB, social security number, driver's license number). Home address (number and apartment/lot number, street, city, state, zip code). Home telephone number, including area code. Occupation (type of work, work hours, days off). Place of employment (name of company, address, street, office number, city, state, zip code). Business telephone number including area code. Email address, FAX number. Education (number of years of school completed, degrees, names of schools).

Next of Kin/Emergency contact (name of person, sex, race, age, dob, SSN, relationship, home address, home phone, work address, work phone.
Statement made in the City Police Department, Room 1010, Criminal Justice Complex, 201 Justice Avenue, Somewhere, Tennessee 3810-1973.
Day, date, time. Statement made to (name of investigators and ID).
Name of persons present (all investigators, attorneys, doctors).
Questioned by: Name of Investigators.   Typed by: Name of typist.
Interview taped or videoed by: name of operator.
This statement is being taken relative to the (type of crime) of (name of victim, sex, race, age) which occurred at (location) on (day, date, time).
Report or Identifier number.

Q: Did you witness a (type of crime)?
A:

Q: Where did this incident occur?
A:

Q: Where were you when the (incident) occurred?
A:

Q: Who did you see (shoot, stab, beat) (name of victim)?
A:

NOTE: When you go to another page put the Report number, Name of Victim, and Page number at the top of the page.

Q: Describe the suspect?
A:

Q: Was the suspect armed?
A:

Q: Describe the weapon.
A:

Q: What did the suspect do with the weapon after the incident?
A:

Q: Where did the suspect go after the incident?
A:

Q: How did the suspect leave the scene?
A:

Q: Who left with the suspect?
A:

Q: Describe this person.
A:

Q: Who else was involved in this incident?
A:

Q: What is your relationship to the suspect?
A:

Q: How long have you known the suspect?
A:

Q: Who was present before the incident occurred?
A:

Q: Who was present during the incident?
A:

Q: Who was present after the incident?
A:

Q: Who saw this incident occur?
A:

Q: What was happening between the suspect and the victim before the incident?
A:

Q: What happened between the suspect and victim during the incident?
A:

Q: Why did the suspect attack the victim?
A:

Q: Do you know the victim?
A:

Q: Who was with the victim?
A:

Q: Was the victim armed?
A:

Q: What is your relationship with the victim?
A:

Q: Tell me in your own words how this incident happened.
A:

Q: Is there anything you wish to add to this statement?
A:

Q: Can you read without the aid of eyeglasses?
A:

Signature of the person giving the statement (all originals should be signed in red)

Signature of all witnesses present

Date: _________________________ Day: _______________ Time: _____

NOTE:

Have the witness initial the bottom of each page and initial each correction in the statement. This should be done in red ink.

Let the witness elaborate about arguments, fights, or whatever they wish. Develop the full series of events preceding and up to the time the victim was removed from the scene.

If the suspect is not in custody ask the witness if they know where the suspect lives, works, or hangs out. Has the witness been in contact with the suspect since the incident? Who might know the location of the suspect?

If a weapon has been recovered, have the witness identify the weapon if possible.

This is only a guideline, attempt to obtain as much information as possible that may lead to other witnesses, suspects, evidence, scenes, or other information.

Defendant note

If the defendant does not wish to make a statement, note the day, date, and time of the refusal and names and point of contact of all persons present. Note the defendant's physical appearance, mood (hostile, passive, unconcerned, nervous), eye contact, body movements, and any utterances. Miranda provides protection of a suspect's 5th Amendment Rights and the suspect does not have to answer questions. It does not mean you cannot make statements or speak to the suspect. Miranda means an investigator cannot ask questions. An investigator may tell the suspect why he is a suspect and the evidence to convict him of a crime. This is a sensitive method and should only be used by a skilled investigator to possibly provoke the suspect into a spontaneous utterance. If a suspect invokes Miranda, keep the recorder going until the suspect has cleared the room.[3,4,5] Somewhere in the suspect's statement the typist should intentionally make a mistake. The suspect must read the statement and make any corrections in red ink. When the suspect discovers the mistake, makes a correction, and initials in red ink it provides evidence that the suspect did read the statement.

Defendant's Statement

Statement of (suspect's full name, sex, race, alias, age, DOB, SSN).

Home address (including city, state, zip code).

Home phone (including area code)

Education (last grade of school completed)

Occupation (type of work)

Employer (name of business, business address, business phone, supervisor's name)

Next-of-kin/emergency contact; Name, sex, race, age, DOB, SSN, home address, home phone, business address, business phone.

Relationship to suspect (mother, father, wife, child, aunt).

Statement made in the City Police Department, Room 1010, 201 Justice Avenue, Somewhere Tennessee 38103-1973 on (day, date, time) to (name of Investigators, must be two present, and any others present) (if Juvenile made in presence of (mother, father, legal guardian, Juvenile Court Representative).

---

[3] The Supreme Court voted 6-3 in Vega v. Tekoh to ensure that many suspects who are denied warnings, commonly known as Miranda Rights, will have no legal recourse against law enforcement, if they are wrongly convicted.

[4] Miranda exclusions questions that are standard booking procedures, emergency hostage situation, the questions are necessary for preserving public safety, the person voluntarily agreed to meet and speak with the police, and the conversation is being taped in secret, jail house informant exception, and others.

[4] In Hiibel v. Sixth Judicial Dist. Court of Nev., Humboldt Cty., 542 U.S. 177 (2004) if state law requires identifying yourself to an officer, refusing to answer a request for one's name during a stop could lead to an arrest.

Questioned by: Name of Investigator

Typed/recorded by: Name of person

(Complete name of suspect in all caps) You are under arrest and will be charged with (type of crime), this charge growing out the (robbery, rape, murder, theft) of (name of victim in all caps, sex, race, age, home address), which occurred on (day, date, time) at (location of crime). Report Number

****

Miranda Advisement

You have the right to remain silent. You do not have to make a statement. Anything you say can and will be used against you in a court of law. You have the right to have an attorney, either of your own choice or court-appointed if you cannot afford one, and to talk with your attorney before answering any questions, and have your attorney with you during questioning if you wish.

Q: Do you understand each of these rights I have explained to you?
A:

Q: Having these rights in mind, do you wish to talk with us now?
A:

Q: Who is the man/woman you (shot, stabbed, struck)?[6]
A:

Q: What kind of weapon did you use?
A:

Q: How many times did you (shoot, stab, strike) (name of victim)?
A:

---

[6] Do not use the words murder, kill. If it is a rape investigation use the term "have sex with".

Q: Who was present when this incident occurred?[7]
A:

Q: Where did this incident occur?[8]
A:

(Page 2 should include: (Defendant's name all in caps, S/R/A Report Number)

Q: What time did this incident occur?
A:

Q: What day did this incident occur?
A:

Q: What date did this incident occur?
A:

Q: What is your relationship with (victim's name)?
A:

Q: Where did you get the gun, knife, club, etc. (or materials) you used?
A:

Q: Who owns this weapon?
A:

Q: What did you do with the weapon after this incident?
A:

Q: Did (name of victim) have a weapon?
A:

---

[7] This question is asked to help locate witnesses.

[8] The crime may have been committed at another location unknown to investigators.

Q: Describe (victim's) weapon?
A:
(Page 3 should include: (Defendant's name all in caps, S/R/A Report Number)
ber)

Q: Who did you tell about this incident?
A:

Q: What is your relationship with (name of victim)?
A:

Q: What was happening between you and (victim's name) before you (shot, beat, raped) (victim's name)?
A:

Q: What did you do after the incident?
A:

Q: Were you injured during this incident?
A:

Q: Tell me in your own words everything about this incident.
A:

Q: Is there anything you wish to add to this statement?
A:

Q: Can you read and write without the aid of eyeglasses?
(If the defendant cannot read his statement have someone not involved in the investigation read it to him. Identify this person on the statement at this point, and have this person sign below.
A:

Q: Can you hear without the use of a hearing aid?
A:

Q: I will ask you to read this statement, consisting of three and three quarters pages, and if you find this statement to be true and correct, as given by you, to sign your name in the lower right hand corner of all pages on the line provided, along with the date and time. Do you understand?
A:

(Page 4 should include: (Defendant's name all in caps, S/R/A Report Number)

Defendant's signature, date, and time_________________________________
Signature of person reading statement._________________________________
Signature of persons in attendance._________________________________ -

____

    Interviewing is an art form that takes training, patience, and experience. Interrogation is a more aggressive form of interviewing. Interviews are used in an investigation to collect information by asking open-ended questions and allowing the witness to supply the evidence. Interrogations are designed to extract confessions where investigators already have other evidence connecting the suspect to the crime. *Advanced Interviewing Techniques* (Shaffer & Navarro, 2010) provides methods for identifying deception in written statements called Text Bridges.[9] Clues can be found in written statements that indicate deception or lies by the word used in the statement explaining the incident. This is a very valuable tool for an investigator. Interviews should be carefully planned after all available information about the incident has been collected by the investigators. Time and place of the interview should be considered. One-on-one interviews have the highest probability of success with no more than two investigators present (Shaffer & Navarro, 2010). Forensic Psychology is a growing method

____

[9] "The most commonly used Text Bridges include *then, so, after, when, as, while, and next*" (Shaffer & Navarro, 2010, p. 100)

of assisting investigators and assessing statements. "Forensic psychologist have developed ways (albeit not foolproof) of distinguishing different types of confessions, including false confessions" (Taylor, 2019, p.3). Text bridges also expose deception.

Listening and observing with an objective but suspicious mind can alert an investigator when a victim is being deceptive about an incident. Often an experienced investigator will sense when something appears out-of-place and a victim or suspect is avoiding the truth. A scene should be examined from several perspectives and viewed in totality.

Investigators received a call regarding a home invasion with shots fired, but no injuries. Investigators arrived on the scene and met the victim (home owner) who advised that three armed men entered his home by the front door. The victim ran to another room as the suspects were making entry. The suspects shot at the victim several times and then turned and ran back out the front door. The victim called police.

Investigators checked with dispatch and learned several calls about shots being fired were received from the neighbors, but the victim did not call until eight minutes after the neighbors. While one investigator interviewed the victim other investigators began checking the house and surrounding area for evidence. An investigator noted bullet holes in the wall and above the door to the room where the victim had run. The investigator also saw bullet holes in the wall and above the front door where the suspects had run out of the house. Another investigator discovered that a wounded male had showed up at the local hospital with gunshot wounds and died in the ER. The gunshot victim was identified by a driver's license and other ID on his person. The gunshot victim had arrests for drug possession and distribution. The home owner had been arrested for simple possession on three occasions.

Inv: Tell me what happened.

Home Owner: I was in the living room watching TV when I heard something at the front door and three men with guns broke through the door and began shooting, *and then* I ran into the bedroom.

Inv: Did the suspects say anything?
Home Owner: No, they just started shooting.

Inv: Did you say anything to the suspects?
Home Owner: *Well,* I would have but didn't have time.

Inv: Did you know or recognize any of the suspects?
Home Owner. I have never seen any of them.

There were two other people present in the home (1 man, 1 woman) when the incident began. They could not provide any additional information and could not identify the suspects. Their statements were vague and both appeared very nervous. There was no damage to the front door indicating a break-in. Other investigators were canvassing the area checking trash cans, dumpsters, interviewing neighbors, checking calls to dispatch, offense and traffic reports to build background on everyone involved. Suspects, victim, and witnesses. The home owner, woman, and man were taken to the investigator's office for statements.

Investigators doing preliminary background on all concerned found the woman had been in a car with the wounded suspect when he had an accident the year before. This established the woman did know the suspect and was lying. The home owner had been arrested two years earlier with the suspect on misdemeanor drug charges, proving the suspect was known to the victim. During the woman's interview she admitted the suspects had come to the home to collect a drug debt owed by the home owner. Investigators questioned the home owner and after being presented with the evidence the home owner stated what happened. The home owner owed money to the suspect for drugs and when the suspect and his friends arrived at the house the owner let them in the front door. An argument ensued between the suspect and the owner. The owner pulled a pistol and ordered the men out of the house. The suspect pulled a pistol and began firing at the home owner who returned fire as the suspects fled out the front door. The home owner's pistol was recovered and ballistics showed a match to the bullet removed from the suspect. All parties were charged with various offenses. Can a victim be a suspect? Yes. Suspect everyone, believe nothing, check everything.

Chapter 4

Authority and Legitimacy

"Legitimacy is a feature of legal systems that makes them worthy of respect, so that people living in legitimate legal systems have reasons to accept the use of state coercion to enforce laws that they do not necessarily agree with and may even think quite unjust. Thus, legitimacy means respect-worthiness..." (Balkin, 2004, p. 486).

An investigator is given authority by the State, but legitimacy is given by the people. "Law enforcement officers are more effectively able to carry out their duties and responsibilities if they are perceived as having legitimate authority by the citizenry that they serve" (Rand, n.d., p. 1). Police legitimacy in urban areas has waned in the 21st century and the separation between police and public has grown wider. The key to closing the gap between officers and the community is through community policing on the model of a small-town police department as opposed to a large urban/metropolitan department. Officers in small towns are more connected to the community than officers in large departments. A small town police department lacks the resources and manpower of large departments, but officer and citizens have close, regular contact and conversations, and this results in a higher clearance rate percentage in small towns. Small town officers usually live in or near the town and have known the people for a long time, "the small-town police department's greatest strength (is) community connectedness" (Falcone et al., 2002, p. 376). It is a lack of connectedness in large police departments that diminishes police legitimacy.

The small town police department's effectiveness is from the departments close relationship with the community, open channels of communication, a lower militarized image, a low bureaucratic hierarchy, work as generalist instead of specialist (Falcone, et. al., 2002).

A uniform officer in a small rural community patrolled a minority community for a number of years. The officer would take elderly sick people to doctor appointments, go to local school ballgames, stop and talk with people in the neighborhood, and helped the residents in many ways. The officer was not a stranger to the community but a respected member of the community. An elderly lady in the neighborhood would sit on her front porch most days and the officer would stop by, sit on the porch, and talk with the lady. They became good friends. The officer was eventually promoted to Investigator and was not in the neighborhood as often as when in uniform patrol, but the officer still maintained a presence and connectedness with the community. A shooting took place in the neighborhood and the uniform officers assigned to the area responded but could not get any information about the suspect from anyone. The former uniform officer now promoted Investigator went to the scene and was greeted cordially by everyone, and he was able to collect information about the incident. While he was in the neighborhood he stopped by the elderly lady's house to check on her and then returned to the office. The phone on his desk started ringing and people were calling to speak with him to tell the identity of the suspect, and an arrest was soon made. An investigator only has legitimacy when it is granted by the community being served, "...a constitutional/legal system is legitimate when all reasonable members of the political community can assent to the content of the constitutional/legal system as they reasonably understand and interpret it... some individuals will refuse to engage in the necessary interpretive charity, and others will simply not be reasonable" (Balkin, 2003, p. 494).

Uniform patrol officers spend several years working in a neighborhood before being promoted to Investigator. This is an opportunity for officers to build a connectedness to that community that can benefit the officers after they become investigators. The bond between an officer and the community he serves is strengthened by frequent visits to the community just to say hello and see how things are going. Trust and respect produce legitimacy.[10] Cooperation of citizens is essential in any police action be it uniform patrol or criminal investigations. Cooperation is founded on the communities perception of police legitimacy. This is the belief that "authorities have the moral right to administer and enforce the law and that people are obligated to obey the law" (Bolger & Walters, 2019, p. 93).

Police procedures have great impact on how a community views the legitimacy of a police agency to enforce the law. Legitimacy is not gained by authoritative power alone but also by the acceptance of the people under that authority.[11] Procedural justice is the foundation of legitimacy and is more easily achieved in small town police departments because of the closeness of the community with the officers. "When people feel a sense of moral solidarity with the police, their sense of identity moves from the individual to the group" (Jackson, et. al., 2012, p. 6). Solidarity is how legitimacy is achieved, but is based on police becoming part of the community and the community becoming part of the police.

The method for connecting with the community in a positive way includes a department wide effort. According to Brown and Benedict:

> ...all personnel — telephone operators, line officers, detectives, supervisors and administrators —should concentrate on conducting themselves in a courteous and professional manner at all times, because there is no dispute in the literature about the effects of perceived inappropriate police behaviors. Owing to the growth of camcorders, roving news helicopters, the media, and the Internet, even an isolated incident of inappropriate police activity can be publicized and create a public relations nightmare. Officers should be aware that their every move is under public scrutiny and that even minor indiscrepancies can do damage to the reputation

---

[10] "Trust is the glue of life. It's the most essential ingredient in effective communication. It's the foundational principle that holds all relationships" (Stephen Covey, 1932-2012).

[11] "Research...indicates that evaluations of police legitimacy are based more on how police treat people than on how well they perform their job" (Murphy, et. al., 2008, p. 140).

of the police. Administrators should strive to promote profession-alism, investigate complaints, and develop strict policies to mini-mize inappropriate behaviors (2002, p. 569).

All this is how your mother told you to treat people, be polite and respectful to everybody always.

Chapter 5
Searches

"Ask, and it will be given to you; seek, and you will find; knock, and it will be opened to you" (New American Standard Bible, 1995, Matthew 7:7-8).

The most common search patterns in outdoor crime scenes are spiral/circle, strip/line, grid/ zone/quadrant, and pie/wheel. Geomorphology is a forensic method of searching a large rural area.[12] The use of drones and Google Earth should be incorporated into a geomorphic search. "Geomorphology plays a critical role in two areas of geoforensics: searching the land for surface or buried objects and sampling scenes of crime and control locations as evidence" (Ruffell & McKinley, 2014, p. 14).

Two clerks were murdered in a small town post office and as part of the investigation a forensic examination of the area was conducted. Some berries from a tree near the scene and other leaves and dirt were collected and tagged as evidence. A few months later a suspect was arrested at another crime scene. In the suspect vehicle evidence was found connected to the post office murders. The suspect vehicle was examined by forensic investigators and tree berries, grass, dirt and other nature items were recovered from the underside of the vehicle that placed the vehicle at the scene

---

[12] "geographic profiling is an investigative methodology that uses the locations of a connected series of crime to determine the most probable area of offender residence" (Ruffell & McKinley, 2014).

of the post office murders.[13] Plants and soil from the crime scene area can place a suspect or vehicle on the scene of a crime. Plant and soil scientist can be found at most universities and can be a valuable investigative tool in geographic profiling.[14]

Detail documentation of the scene is critical to the investigation. Once officers clear a scene and the crime scene tape comes down it is nearly impossible to introduce evidence into court found after the investigators have left the scene. Searches must be planned, coordinated, and supervised by the lead investigator. Everyone, including officers, on the scene must be documented. There is usually too many people wandering about the scene picking up or finding evidence and not documenting who found what, where. Searches should start at the point of entry or location of the victim. Check air vents, vacuum cleaners, trash, anything and everything that could provide clues. Check commodes, dirty clothes hampers, and anything that may have DNA. "DNA is contained in blood, semen, skin cells, tissue, organs, muscle, brain cells, bone, teeth, hair, saliva, mucus, perspiration, fingernails, urine, feces, etc" (United States Department of Justice [n.d.]). A crime scene technician was directed by an investigator to take samples from a commode of feces and urine in the bathroom of a homicide victim. The technician resisted taking the samples because it was repulsive. Another technician was called to the scene and took the samples. Those samples connected the suspect to the murder and led to his conviction in court.

Crime scenes should be large enough to include possible avenues of approach or departure of the suspect or any possible use of transportation or communication. Officers responded to a homicide scene where the victim was found in the cab of his 18-wheeler with two gunshot wounds. The uniform patrol officers on the scene had enclosed a very narrow area around

---

[13] "One hundred years ago Georg Popp became the first scientist to present in court a case where the geological makeup of soils was used to secure a criminal conviction" (Ruffell & McKinley, 2005, p. 235).

[14] "Geographic profiling is an investigative support technique for serial violent crime investigations. The process analyzes locations connected to a series of crimes to determine the most probable area in which the offender lives. Geographic profiling should be regarded as an information management system designed to help focus an investigation, prioritize tips and suspects, and suggest new strategies to complement traditional methods" (Texas State Center for Geospatial Intelligence and Investigation, n.d.).

the truck as the scene, which was in a vacant lot in the rear of a fast food shop. Investigators expanded the crime scene tape up to the rear of the shop. Inside this area was a phone booth. Crime scene technicians obtained prints from a soda can in the phone booth. The phone company was contacted and a record of calls from the phone was obtained. The crouch of the victim's pants contained what appeared to be semen and salvia. The prints from the soda can and the phone booth identified a known prostitute and a call made from that phone went to a known pimp. This information also fixed the time of death of the victim. After the prostitute was arrested a DNA match was made from the saliva on the victim's pants. The victim had refused to pay the prostitute the full amount of money agreed on for her services. She went to the phone booth and called her pimp who came to the scene, confronted and shot the victim. If the crime scene had not been expanded, the fundamental evidence would not have been found leading to the suspects.

The investigation of a rape scene is another example of enlarging the scene because, "potential criminals do not search through a whole city for targets they look for targets within their more restrictive awareness space" (Warren, et.al., 1998, p.39). In many instances the suspect is within 3 miles of the scene. This is why it is important to know the location of all sex offenders. "Research indicates that serial rapists travel on average 3.14 miles to rape but the average shortest/closest distance is 1.66 miles...Half the serial rapist in the research raped victims within 0.5 miles from the rapist residence" (Warren, et. al. 1998, p. 55).

Doctoral students use a number of software programs to help in the analysis of the data collected for their dissertation research. These same programs can benefit a criminal investigator. These programs can help to systematically evaluate and interpret texts in statements and investigative notes and is useful in developing theories and testing conclusions. A few of the programs are MAXQDA, ATLAS.ti, NVivo, and *Hyper*RESEARCH in addition to many others.

Chapter 6

The Power of Language

"Words have a magical power. They can either bring the greatest happiness or the deepest despair" (Sigmund Freud, 1856-1939).

When interviewing a suspect the choice of words can determine whether or not a reliable statement of admission (confession) will be acquired. The typical interview/interrogation of a suspect is accusatorial because, "entrenched, belief that an accusatorial approach—and sometimes even more coercive methods—is the most effective strategy for interrogating a suspect or a source" (Brimbal, et. al., 2019, p. 5). The accusatorial approach has produced some negative results in the past resulting in false confessions that degrade the integrity and legitimacy of the department. A suspect interview should be carefully planned, not only the questions to be asked, but staging the environment. These things will be different with each case because each case and the people involved are unique.

An interview is nonaccusatory and people are more likely to answer questions if they believe they are not being accused of committing a crime. This should be the first approach used in questioning a suspect. An interrogation is accusatory and puts the suspect in a defensive posture and he will usually invoke Miranda. There are exceptions to advising a suspect of Miranda (5th Amendment) rights. An interrogation is used to find the truth as does an interview. The difference is in the investigators aggressiveness. An investigator must maintain objectivity during interviews and interrogations. In most cases more can be learned from an interview than an interrogation. An investigator should have some background on the victim, witness, and suspect prior to interviewing. This helps an investigator to determine the best approach to use during the interview/interrogation and measure the response of the answers (Inbau, et. al., 2013).

Choose the words of the questions carefully. Instead of saying "Did you murder John Smith" say "Did you shoot/stab/strike John Smith?" Instead of asking "did you rape" someone, ask "did you have sex with…" The choice of words can encourage the suspect to admit to committing some act if the suspect believes the investigators are not condemning him. If the suspect admits to striking John Smith, he is confirming he murdered John Smith. If a suspect admits to having sex with a victim, he is admitting to raping the victim.

This approach differs from the usual aggressiveness in an interrogation by avoiding words that can elicit a defensive attitude from a suspect. "Psychological police interrogation methods in America inevitably involve some level of pressure and persuasion" (Leo & Liu, 2009, p. 381). This is a common perception in law enforcement but the choice of words in an interrogation can circumvent the usual "pressure and persuasion" used to obtain confessions. Using less aggressive language or physical intimidation produces a more cooperative and true confession.

Chapter 7

A Suspicious Mind

"Suspicion often father of truth" Charlie Chan at the Race Track (1936).

A common and necessary trait among criminal investigators is suspicion or curiosity. Police officers are continually scanning the areas they drive through looking at everything and nothing. An officer notices a man standing in front of a house and as the officer passes the man he turns and looks again. The investigator intuition of suspicion has unconsciously alerted the officer that something is not right with this scene. When in doubt check it out. There are times when nothing wrong is found, but in most cases a closer examination will disclose some criminal or deviant behavior. The third principle of conducting a criminal investigation is check everything. This includes everybody involved in a call. Victims and witnesses can be perpetrators and backgrounds of everyone should be checked.

Investigators responded to a robbery call at a pizza store. The clerk was in the store alone preparing to close the business. The day's receipts were on the counter when an armed man entered the store and demanded the money. The perpetrator took the money and fled the scene. The investigator began his interview of the clerk.

Inv: How much money was taken?

Clerk: Six hundred and eighty six dollars. I had just counted it and was about to put it is a bag to drop off at the bank night depository, *and then*[15] a man came through the door with a gun.

Inv: Who else was in the store?

Clerk: No one. I had let everybody leave.

Inv: Describe the suspect.

Clerk: (He provided a vague description of a large man wearing a black hoody and gloves armed with a gun).

Inv: Describe the gun.

Clerk: I don't know much about guns, it was big, and black?

Inv: Which hand did the suspect have the gun in?

Clerk: I don't remember.

Inv: What about the surveillance video?

Clerk: I had just taken out the tape to put in a new one so there is no video.

Inv: Did the suspect come through the door after you removed the video?

Clerk: *Well*[16], I had just added up the money and was about to put it in the deposit bag, *and then* the guy came in with a gun and said "give me all the money". I handed it to him and he ran out the door.

Inv: Can you identify the suspect if you see him again?

Clerk: Maybe, I don't know.

15Text bridges, indicates information is missing. (Schaffer & Navarro, 2010, p. 100).

16 Direct questions need yes or no answers. "If the answer begins with the word "well", there is a high probability of deception" (Schaffer & Navarro, 2010, p. 111).

Inv: Do you have any money on you?
Clerk: Yes, about five bucks.

Inv: Just to eliminate any possible suspicion, empty your pockets on the counter.
Clerk: Placed everything on the counter and he had five dollars and some change.

Another investigator came in and whispered something to the interviewing investigator.

Inv: Do you have a car outside?
Clerk: Yeah, why?

Inv: We would like to look inside your car.
Clerk: Do you have a warrant?

Inv: No, but we don't need one if you give your permission.
Clerk: I don't want you all in my car.

Inv: Ok. My partner is going for a warrant, so we will all wait here till he gets back.
Clerk: Are you accusing me of taking the money?

Inv: Did you?
Clerk: You're going to look in my car aren't you?

Inv: Yes.
Clerk: Ok, the money's in the trunk.

There are several things in the investigator's interview with the clerk that aroused suspicion. The first is a text bridge in the clerk's opening comments (*and then*). Second, the clerk had released the other employees before preparing a bank deposit.[17] Third, leaving the door unlocked before counting the day's receipts. Fourth, removing the video before securing and closing the store. Fifth, the vagueness of a suspect description. Sixth, the overall demeanor of the clerk and his refusal to allow inspection of his car. The interviewing investigator's partner checked on the clerk while the interview was being done. The clerk had been arrested twice on misdemeanor drug charges, and once for D.U.I. Offense reports were also checked and showed the clerk had been robbed twice before at two different stores under the same circumstances with very similar suspect descriptions. No arrest had been made in these robberies. Even victims and/or witnesses can become suspects. Objectivity and suspicion are good case closers. Suspect everybody, believe nothing, check everything.

---

[17] These employees will need to be located and statements taken.

Chapter 8
Perception and Projection

"All things are subject to interpretation. Whichever interpretation prevails at a given time is a function of power and not truth." (Friedrich Nietzsche, 1844-1900).

An investigator must take care with his personal appearance and public demeanor lest the public perceives him as incompetent, arrogant, oppressive, and insincere. Most law enforcement agencies have standards on personal appearance in a policy and procedure manual and these standards will vary between agencies. These personal appearance standards have been relaxed over the years reflecting a change of culture and generation. Most law enforcement agencies will agree that police officers/investigators should project a professional, business, and confident image. What should that image be is the question?

The issue is discussed by examining two publications. One written in 1994 and the other in 2017. The grooming standards for law enforcement officers in the 20th century were more restrictive than standards for today. However, even then there were varying degrees of permissiveness from department to department. The Los Angeles Police Department maintained strict standards from haircuts to clothing. The New York Police Department was more flexible and the differences can be seen in photographs of officers in the two departments during those years. In some departments grooming standards were written in detail in a policy and other departments had no written standards but expectations.

The 21st century grooming standards for officers reflects the social behavior and culture of the day. Generally, anything is permissible with perhaps the exception of facial tattoos and piercings. This also varies among departments. In 1976 the U.S. Supreme Court in *Kelley v Johnson* "ruled that the police department demonstrated a rational connection between the department's grooming regulation and the promotion of safety of persons and property. Thus, the regulation was not in violation of the 14th amendment's due process liberty protections" (McCormack, 1994, p. 27). The issue of grooming standards for police officers in 1976 was enforced by Kelly v Johnson giving departments wide discretion in establishing and enforcing grooming standards. According to McCormack, "Courts have granted law enforcement managers broad discretion in determining what grooming standards are appropriate for their department or agency" (1994, p. 30). This ruling has been upheld in similar cases, Jespersen v. Harrah's Operation's Code, Seabrook v. City of New York, Riggs v. City of Fort Worth, and others, "the courts clearly and repeatedly took the stance that employers may in fact dictate grooming policies as long as they are fair, consistently applied, and do not violate Title VII of the Civil Rights Act of 1964" (Midkiff, 2020, p.7).

Officers displaying tattoos in the 20th century was generally prohibited, especially if those tattoos were visible. Piercings were out of the question and beards were not permitted. Recent research reveals that tattoos are associated with deviant behavior, e.g. gang membership, drug use, carrying weapons, and overall trustworthiness making tattoos disturbing to citizens. However, according to Trimming and Perrett:

> …as more and more people get tattooed it is arguable that the 'counter-cultural' meanings associated with body art are becoming gradually diluted. Similarly, the increased prevalence of body art may also have diminished perceptions of a potential association between tattoos and delinquency, and therefore violence (2017, p. 125).

Community policing guidelines recommend that officers mirror the culture and social acuity of the communities they police. "Social acuity has been identified as an important skill in promoting positive interpersonal and psychological functioning" (Aube & Whiffen, 1996, p 407). This reasoning would imply that if tattoos, piercings, and beards are prevalent in the community then officers would be more acceptable to citizens if their appearance was similar. A criminal investigator should present an appearance and demeanor that exemplifies competence, fairness, trust, and professionalism.

Chapter 9

Writing It Up

"Remembrance of things past is not necessarily the remembrance of things as they were" (Marcel Proust, 1871-1922).

Documentation of a criminal investigation must be done as the case develops and be thorough, complete, comprehensive, understandable and not left to memory.[18] Statements, evidence, and investigator actions clearly connect and support the findings of the investigation. The following is a simple and basic format for documenting the case:

SUPPLEMENT SUBMITTED BY: Sgt. Carl Q. Doe, IBM 0001, Car 1656
Saturday, August 15, 2010 – 0345 Hours
Report Number 980800222 (Homicide, etc.)

VICTIM (S):
Full Name, Sex, Race, Age D/O/B, SS#, H/A (Including city state, zip code.) H/P, Occupation, Employed by (Name of business) business address and business phone, cell number and email address.
List victim's injuries (if any).
Victim can or cannot identify suspect.
List subsequent victims and QW each.

---

[18] "the power or process of reproducing or recalling what has been learned and retained especially through associative mechanisms" (Merriam Webster)

Note if Victim(s) armed.

Clothing and physical description of victim(s) such as tattoos, scars, gold teeth, etc.

Next of Kin.

SUBJECT (S):

Full Name, (if known), Race, Sex, Age, D/O/B (if known), SS#, (if known) alias/nickname, height, weight, build, complexion, hair (style, color, long, short), facial hair (mustache/bread), clothing description, H/A/, H/P, Occupation, Employed by, business address and telephone, cell number, email address.

NOTE: If suspect is not in custody the witnesses' description may vary. Include all variations. Do not make a composite.

DAY/DATE/TIME/LOCATION OF OCCURRENCE:

The day of the week, the date of month, year, approximate time it occurred, and the location.

WITNESSES:

All information listed in Victim paragraph should also be listed for each witness.

Verify their identity.

Run a QW on each.

List the Next of Kin.

NEXT OF KIN:

Full name, race, sex, age, D/OB/, SS#, H/A, H/P, cellular, pager, name of employer, business address and telephone, relation to victim.

Notified or not notified.

Advised of pending autopsy, by whom, date, time, and location where notified. Must be made in person. D/O/A victim must be identified by next of kin or family member.

NOTE: All natural deaths, where a doctor will not sign the death certificate, must go to the morgue for the Medical Examiner.

All accidental deaths, suicides, and homicides must be sent to the morgue for the Medical Examiner.

BODY REMOVAL SERVICE:

The Investigator must obtain body removal attendants' initials, last name, and the Unit Number transporting, along with the date and time they arrive to transport the body.

If the victim expires at The Med no information is needed regarding the transporting services as the Med has their own.

SCENE OFFICERS:

Rank, name, IBM #, Car and Shift #

Need to obtain first car on scene, what time they received call, to what location, and time of arrival and what type call.

If any uniform officer has picked up any evidence on the scene that officer is to tag the property and notify crime scene where it has been located on the scene. If any officer/person has made any adjustments to scene identify that officer/person and the adjustments they made.

List officers according to rank, i.e. Major Lieutenant, etc.

Note: If the victim has been transported prior to the Investigator's arrival at the scene, the Investigator should ask the uniform officers if the victim was there when they arrived and if so, what position his body was in and where it was located. If victim is moved prior to uniform officers' arrival, the Investigator should send another Investigator or go to the hospital himself to obtain information on kind of injuries victim sustained.

INVESTIGATIVE OFFICERS:
Rank, name, IBM #, Car, and Shift #
(Same order as uniform officers.)

EMERGENCY RESPONSES:
Fire Department Unit #, Names, IBM #s and Duty Position, i.e., Paramedic, EMT, Driver.
Their call time and scene time should be obtained and location of call.
Doctors or Nurses on duty at ER.
Morgue attendant's name.

WEAPONS:

Description of weapon, i.e., gun, knife, bottle, etc. Any serial numbers or identifying marks and which suspect was armed with this weapon. Should be same information on victim's weapon.

Run N.C.I.C. check and name of person running check, date, and time.

Note: If weapon is recovered on the scene, the Investigator should be with the crime scene officer when the weapon is inspected. If it is a revolver, show how many spent and live rounds are in the cylinder and if round is under the hammer has been fired.

If weapon is semi-automatic, how many rounds in magazine, if a round is in the chamber, and how many rounds does the magazine hold. Attempt to get fingerprints from the rounds in the magazine or chamber of the weapon.

The same applies to shotguns and rifles.

If the weapon is a handgun, record the barrel length, color, type and color of grips, brand name, serial number, model number of weapon, type and name of ammunition of each live and spent round.

If the weapon is a shotgun, single or double barrel, length of barrel, color of barrel and stock, and overall length. Same applies to a rifle, along with the other identifying descriptions as that of the handgun.

If the weapon is a knife, sword, bayonet, screw-driver, etc., list the length of the blade and the overall length; describe the handle, and what type knife or sword.

VEHICLES:

Model, Year, Make, description i.e., color, number of doors, stickers, damage, license number, VIN, if possible, N.C.I.C. check and registration. Disposition, i.e., left at scene, towed to lot or crime scene tunnel to be processed, by whom. Need name of wrecker service, address, phone #, and the driver's name, D/O/B, SS#, H/A/, H/P, page, cellular.

This applies to both the victim and the suspect vehicles.

PROPERTY TAKEN:

If more than one victim, list property taken from each individual, along with the description and value of each item taken.

List amount of money taken, in what denominations, serial numbers, any credit cards, checks, etc.

PROPERTY RECOVERED:

Any property recovered should be photographed and processed for prints. A description of each item recovered should be given. The location where it was found and the name of the owner, if possible.

LIGHTING CONDITIONS:

Poor or good, daylight, moonlight, street light. Lights on or off. Above should apply to outside scenes. Kind of lighting inside residence, lamps, overhead, or wall mounts, and bulb wattage.

Note: If no lights are on inside residence, check for lighting from outside source.

WEATHER CONDITION:

Temperature, Hot, Cold, Wet, Dry, Cloudy, Clear, Raining, Snowing/Sleeting, etc.

SCENE: (This should be a detailed written description as seen by the Investigator and photographed by both still and video photography.)

If the homicide occurs inside an apartment, duplex, or house the Investigator should start the description with the direction the street runs (north, south, east, west); the nearest intersection and what direction it is from the scene; the addresses or unit numbers on each neighbor on both sides; which side of the street the resident is located on; which direction the residence faces the street; location of front and rear door; single, two story dwelling; wood frame, brick, etc., color or wood, brick, etc., and trim; location of driveway. There may be some variations in the description of a house, i.e., porch, carport, garage (type door and if garage is attached or separate from house), common or separate porch for duplex.

If the homicide is inside the residence, describe the interior of the house, listing the direction you are traveling as you enter; number of rooms i.e., living room, den, kitchen, hallway, stairs, baths, and bedroom locations.

Described the condition of the room where the homicide occurred i.e. clean, dirty, cluttered, or if any sign of a struggle or fight having taken place. Describe any blood found at any location inside the residence; try to determine where the initial altercation started and where the victim's body fell.

In the room where the victim was found, a description of the contents of the room and the location of these items in relation to the location of the body. Also, any evidence found in the room where the body is located as well as any physical evidence in the room where the initial altercation began. You should stand at an opening or doorway where the body is visible and list the contents of the room from left to right or right to left.

The body should be described as to which direction the head and feet are pointing. Describe how the body is lying, i.e., on the back with face up, on the side, or on the stomach with the face down or to which side. Describe the position the legs and arms are laying, i.e., bent at knees, spread, toe up, palms up or down, by side or bent at elbow and extended out from the body, etc.

The body should also be described as a whether rigor mortis is present; any lividity is seen; body temperature i.e. warm or cold, if possible; visible wound or wounds; location of any blood around the body; what the victim was wearing; was there a weapon present. If the weapon is a knife or any other type instrument note whether the weapon is still in the body, where it is located, and do not remove. If it is a gunshot wound, establish whether or not there is an entrance and exit wound. This will enable the Investigator to know whether or not a search should be made for a spent projectile at the scene.

The Investigator should be with the Crime Scene Officer when any property is removed from the victim's body, i.e. jewelry, money, identification, etc. Check every pocket in the victim's clothing and list each item taken from each pocket.

Any weapon found in and around the area where the body is located should be described as to which direction the weapon is pointing, where the weapon is in relation to the victim, what type weapon, color length, and if the weapon is a gun the Investigator should be present when the Crime Scene officer checks for spent and live ammunition and the location they are in the weapon. Any spent casings found around the body should be documented as to the location in relation to the body. Any spent casing or live rounds found on the scene should be processed for fingerprints.

When the body is removed, the clothing should be left intact and sent to the morgue. If the paramedics have cut any of the clothing off the body, it should be tagged by Crime Scene. If the body has been wrapped in a sheet, rug, plastic bag, etc., it should not be disturbed, but sent to the morgue as it is.

If the victim is listed as critical on the scene and could possibly expire the Investigator should follow the same procedure as that of a homicide. Should family members be present on the scene get one to identify victim; also, if the victim is DOA on the scene the Investigator should notify them of the pending autopsy. If the family member is not the next of kin the Investigator can still advise him of the pending autopsy. If victim has not yet expired try to obtain the name of next of kin. The Investigator should note the day, date, and time of notification, as well as the day, date, and time of identification. If the body has not been identified by a family member, prior to being sent to the morgue, next of kin should be located and have the person met you at the morgue, after ascertaining the body can be viewed. The day, date, and time the body is identified should be noted as well as notifying the person of the pending autopsy.

If the victim expires at the hospital, the Investigator should go there and ascertain who pronounced the victim and the time of death. Also, if the victim's clothing has been removed, have Crime Scene come to the hospital, obtain the clothing, and tag it as evidence the property room.

If the victim's personal property has been removed by hospital personnel and tagged, identify the person who removed the property and anyone else who may have handled the property. The Investigator will obtain and tag the property as personal.

While on the scene, if someone has assisted the victim in some way, i.e., placing a pillow under the head, using a sheet or blanket to cover, a towel, etc., this should be noted and tagged by crime scene as evidence. Identify the person who assisted the victim.

In a suicide involving a firearm the hands of the victim should be placed in paper bags by the crime scene. If the homicide victim has a firearm or was seen using a firearm the hands should be bagged by the crime scene prior to being sent to the morgue. If identification of the deceased is an issue then fingerprints will be taken by the crime scene officers and the hands will not be bagged.

The victim of a homicide or suicide should have his thumb print taken to be identified through R & I, unless his hands have been bagged for a gunshot residue test, even if he has been identified on the scene. In cases where the victim has no identification on them a full set of prints should be obtained by the Investigator and run through the R & I Section to see if they have a previous record. This enables the victim to be identified and possibly will help to locate the next of kin. If this information is obtained the Investigator should note the day, time and name of the technician providing information. If there are any eyewitnesses to the homicide or critical victim they are to be brought to the office and a typed statement obtained. If the witness refuses to cooperate check with the Attorney General or Legal Adviser before placing the witness under arrest.

Other witnesses, who have very little information to give, can be interviewed on the scene and an oral statement obtained and possibly recorded for later transcription. The statement should be included in the supplement, noting the time of the interview and all pertinent information regarding this witness (the witness should sign and note the date and time). This also applies to critical victims. Get positive identification of witnesses and run a QW.

In the case of a suicide, if the weapon is some type of gun, it should be handled the same way as a homicide. If it involves drugs list all medication found at the scene, who prescribed it, the pharmacy where it was filled, and note the quantity prescribed and quantity left in the bottles. This medication is to be placed in an envelope by the crime scene officer and sent in the body bag to the morgue for the Medical Examiner. The same applies to any syringes located at the scene. If the victim is being treated by a physician get the name, address, and phone number. If the victim is being cared for by more than one physician, obtain the same information on all of them.

If it is a suicide by hanging, the rope, cord, etc., should be cut at the location where it is tied and left intact on the body and sent to the morgue with the victim. Neither the knot at the neck or location where it is attached to an object should be untied. Leave all knots intact.

In the case of a suicide, the wife, husband, or a family member on the scene should be brought to the office for a typed statement. Also, if a note is found it is to be tagged as evidence and processed for fingerprints.

If the victim is found inside a vehicle, the Investigator should describe the location i.e., parking lot, street, driveway, etc. note the direction the front and rear of the vehicle is facing and which side is next to the curb.

Start from outside the vehicle noting if the lights are on or off; motor running; any damage; check exhaust pipe to determine if motor has been recently running; which windows are open or closed; which doors are locked or unlocked; keys in or out of ignition; location of any weapons or other evidence. Describe position of body using same guidelines or any homicide. After the body has been removed from vehicle the same guideline governing personal property removal should be followed.

Child Abuse

If the Investigator should make the scene involving child abuse a Crime Scene Photographer should be called to photograph any injuries to the child. If the Investigator is called to the a home the child needs to be taken to the hospital to determine if medical attention is needed for any injury sustained and have medical personnel document the injuries. A detailed description of the scene should be made, including any physical evidence located.

If it is learned the suspect is the same person reporting the offense or a person living in the same household, the child is to be taken in Protective Custody and not be allowed to return to the same environment where the suspect has control of the victim. Department of Human Services should be notified to see if they want to make the scene and inform them of the information you have obtained. The main concern is to get medical attention for the child if it is needed and insure the child is and will remain in a safe environment. If the agent for DHS wants to meet you, have them go to the hospital. This applies to child rape victims as well as the physical abuse cases.

When the Investigator is sent to a hospital, interview the doctor in charge of the victim and the nurse assigned to the victim. If it is unknown at the time the Investigator is at the hospital whether or not the child will be admitted, the Investigator should contact the hospital to obtain this information before completing the supplement.

Missing Persons:

Thousands of missing persons calls are received by police departments every year. Many are quickly resolved by uniform patrol, but others require the work of criminal investigators. A nineteen-year-old female with a mental disability left her home to go to a nearby grocery store in a small shopping area. The victim had the mental ability of a ten-year-old. There had been no contact with the victim for two hours and the parents had checked the area for the victim without success. Uniform officers arrived on the scene, obtained a description of the victim and checked the area between the victim's home and the shopping area and found nothing. Officers went to the grocery store and checked with the clerks and store surveillance. No one remembered seeing the girl. The store's surveillance video was checked and the girl did not appear in the video. Uniform officers then contacted investigators and advised them of the situation. Investigators arrived at the girl's home, interviewed the parents, and obtained a current picture of the girl. An investigator took the picture to the police photo lab and had several copies made of the picture. These were distributed to other investigators and uniform patrol officers. Additional uniform patrol officers arrived and a door-to-door search for the girl began. Investigators learned the girl had never gone missing before and lived a happy life in the world of a ten-year-old even though she was nineteen. Five hours had passed and no leads as to the girl's disappearance were found. Investigators and officers began checking vacant buildings, ditches, secluded areas, and retraced the possible routes to the grocery store the girl may have taken, no leads. Investigators went to the shopping area and reinterviewed the grocery store clerks and security personnel. The store's surveillance video was viewed from one hour before the girl left home until four hours after, she was not in the video. Six hours had now passed and nothing new had been learned. Investigators began checking the other stores in the shopping area and when they came to a toy store and showed a clerk the girl's picture the clerk remembered her being in the store. Investigators contacted the store security and showed them the girl's picture. The security officers recognized the girl and advised investigators the girl had been arrested for shop lifting.

The store surveillance video was checked and showed the girl looking at dolls, picking a doll up and after looking at it a few moments put the doll under her coat and started walking to the front door where she was arrested. Other investigators checked the jail and found the girl was in custody. Investigators on the scene at the store explained the girl's mental disability and that she had no prior arrest record. The store management decided to sign a Refusal to Prosecute Form dismissing any charges against the girl. Investigators advised the parents the girl was safe and was being brought home. Investigators at the jail obtained the girl's release without charges and transported the girl home. The was talking with investigators during the ride and explained she loved cabbage patch dolls and when she saw the cabbage patch doll in the store it looked cold so she put it under her coat to get it warm and take it home where she could care for it. Investigators at the toy store were informed of the girl's story and after a short discussion bought the Cabbage Patch doll to give to the girl. It seems the investigators at the toy store both had daughters about ten years old.

Missing Persons Investigations

The Investigator should interview the parents or guardian of the child to see who their friends are; the last person who saw the victim; to see if there is a domestic problem over the child, i.e., ex-husband, ex-wife.

The first person the Investigator should interview is the last known person to see the child. It should be determined where and what time the child was seen and who the child may have been seen with.

If this should be a domestic case the other party should be contacted to determine if the child is with them. Also, a uniform car should be sent to that location to ascertain if the child is there. If there is some question as to who has legal custody, the child should be taken to Juvenile Court for Protective Custody.

If the child is not located through friends or relatives, the Investigator and Uniform Officers should search the house and any building on the property to see if the child is possibly hiding. If this does not produce the missing child, try to determine which playmate the child plays with the most. Start at that point and check every residence the parents tell you are her playmates.

While still talking with the parents or guardian of the missing child, the Investigator should have a Uniform Car riding in the neighbor and broadcasting on the car P.A. system, giving the child's name and a description. After all the homes of the playmates you know about have been checked and the child has not been located, then start a house to house search beginning at the child's home, then in both directions as well as the other side of the street.

If there are any parks, playgrounds, or wooded areas near the child's home, a thorough search should be made of these areas. If it is night time the helicopter and a dog car should be call to the scene to help search the area for the child.

The Investigator should check Juvenile Court to see if the child has been picked up and place there on Protective Custody. Have the Dispatcher check with the hospitals to see if an injured child, without a parent or guardian, has come in for treatment.

While canvassing the neighborhood, try to ascertain if the residents have noticed any suspicious people or cars in the neighborhood recently. Determine if any registered Sex Offenders live in the area and immediately make contact with the offenders.

Determine if the missing party has a mental disorder or is on medication; if they are an elderly person who is senile, or has Alzheimer's disease. If the missing person is on medication find out when the next dose is due. Remember that the missing person could be the victim of a kidnapping. In this type of case the guidelines for a kidnapping investigation should be followed.

If a vehicle is known to be involved in a kidnapping or missing person case, if the vehicle is found, check with relatives to see if they have keys to the vehicle. If they do a uniform car should be sent to obtain the keys and return them to the location where the vehicle is. The trunk should be opened without touching the vehicle and if the keys are not located the vehicle should be sent to the crime scene for processing.

Under no circumstances should the scene officers enter or touch the vehicle. However, if possible the trunk should be opened to see if the victim could be there before the vehicle is sent to the crime scene building.

If a suspect is arrested for a homicide, rape, robbery, or has been wounded, their clothing should be taken and tagged as evidence. Be sure to list the name of the person removing the clothing.

Missing Person/Runaway Check List:
Detailed description of victim and current picture if possible
Determine if victim is taking medication
Check Jail for victim
Check impound lots for victim's vehicle
Check Records for previous Missing Person/Runaway reports on victim
Check Credit Cards and checks of victim
Check victim's personal areas for names of friends and phone numbers
Check victim's residence and areas frequented by victim
Check neighborhood
Check area stores victim frequents
Check email and caller ID
Check Juvenile Court if victim is a juvenile
Determine if victim had money
Check victim's home for missing clothes and luggage
Re-check everything

Chapter 10
Case Closed

"Success is the ability to go from failure to failure without losing your enthusiasm" (Winston Churchill, 1874-1965).

Many times an investigation comes to a dead end and try as they may investigators cannot come to a logical or successful conclusion. Identification of a victim is paramount to successfully conducting and closing an investigation. The identity of a victim leads to other sources of information and associations.

An investigator was assigned to the homicide of a middle aged man who was found behind a large clump of bushes next to a church that was adjacent to police headquarters. Homeless people frequently stayed around the church which was an old and large building. The victim was found by a homeless man who did not know the victim by name but had seen him with another younger man in the area on several occasions. Crime scene technicians took the victim's fingerprints at the morgue and ran them through AFIS (Automated Fingerprint Identification System) with negative results. Crime Scene technicians took photographs of the victim and the investigator had several flyers printed and distributed in the area in an attempt to identify the victim. Negative results. The investigator visited a nearby homeless shelter and found several people who knew the victim by sight but not his name. The investigator worked the area through various times of the day and night attempting to find someone who could identify the victim. Negative results. The investigator checked the area businesses' surveillance videos and found the victim in some of the videos walking or talking to other homeless people. Photographs of the other people in the video were made and the investigator again canvassed the area to identify any of the people seen in the video around the victim. A few men were found who had seen the victim in the downtown area and at the homeless shelter but did not know his name. Witnesses stated they often saw the victim with a younger man but did not know his name either.

The investigator reported to the Lieutenant that he had not been able to identify the victim and did not know what else to try. He was at a dead end. The Lieutenant advised the investigator to put everything aside and begin again as if he had just received the call. The investigator restarted his investigation rechecking all the witnesses and evidence. He had crime scene technicians refingerprint the victim and sent the prints to AFIS. This time AFIS provided the name of the victim who had a non-violent criminal record. The investigator checked the jail records and found the victim had been released a few hours before his murder. The jail property receipt for the victim showed he had $111.00 and some change and some other mundane things. The investigator also checked to see who had been released during the same time frame. Photographs and names of the other people released from jail were showed to witness and several people pointed out a younger man as being a regular companion of the victim. An NCIC broadcast was sent out requesting information on the younger man. A few hours later investigators were notified that subject was incarcerated in a town 85 miles away. The investigator and his partner went to the other city to interview the subject. When the subject entered the interview room he stated, "I have been expecting you guys, I know what you are here for." The subject admitted to killing the victim with a rock after an argument over money the victim had. The victim was a Viet Nam Veteran and received a disability check from the VA. The suspect gave the investigators a written statement of admission.

Check everything is the third premise of an investigation. This also means when all else fails start again. Many times new eyes can provide new ideas and inspiration. If a fresh set of the victim's fingerprints had not been resubmitted the case may well still be a mystery.

A criminal investigation is an exhausting and time-consuming effort. Every aspect of the case (arrest report) is scrutinized by several investigators, supervisors, and attorneys, making constant reinvestigation necessary. A conversation with a defense attorney who was a respected adversary of an investigator showed just how significant all the painstaking effort was in a court of law. First, the attorney remarked that the Investigator had done a splendid job with the investigation. The statements from witnesses, perpetrators, experts, and analysts were flawless; the collection of evidence and documentation of the evidence chain was unbreakable; the analysis of evidence, statements, and forensics was expertly done. Then the attorney said, "all your work is immaterial, all I have to do is convince a couple of the jurors my client is innocent, and he walks away. Your work will be marked "case closed" and filed away, so why do you do this job? The Investigator smiled and said, "because it is my mission to "Defend the poor and fatherless; Do justice to the afflicted and needy. Deliver the poor and needy; Free them from the hand of the wicked" (New King James Version, 1982, Plasm 82:3-4).

Case Closed.

References

Aube, J., & Whiffen, V. E. (1996). Depressive styles and social acuity: Further evidence for distinct interpersonal correlates of dependency and self-criticism. *Communication Research, 23*(4), 407-424.
https://journals.sagepub.com/doi/abs/10.1177/009365096023004004

Balkin, J. M. (2003). Respect-worthy: Frank Michelman and the legitimate constitution. *Tulsa L. Rev., 39*, 485. https://digitalcommons.law.utulsa.edu/cgi/viewcontent.cgi?article=2448&context=tlr

Bolger, P. C., & Walters, G. D. (2019). The relationship between police procedural justice, police legitimacy, and people's willingness to cooperate with law enforcement: A meta-analysis. *Journal of criminal justice, 60*, 93-99.
https://www.sciencedirect.com/science/article/abs/pii/S0047235219300029

Branch, Jr. B. (2018, November 8). Police Agencies and Relaxed Grooming Codes: Why We Should Make the Change. Arkansas State University Police Department. https://www.cji.edu/wp-content/uploads/2019/06/police_agencies_and_relaxed_grooming_codes.pdf

Brimbal, L., Kleinman, S. M., Oleszkiewicz, S., & Meissner, C. A. (2019). Developing rapport and trust in the interrogative context: An empirically-supported and ethical alternative to customary interrogation practices. *SJ, Barela, MJ, Fallon, G., Gaggioli, JD Ohlin,(Eds.), Interrogation and torture: Integrating efficacy with law and morality*, 141-196. file:///C:/Users/tn/Downloads/Brimbaletal.inpress.pdf

Brown, B., & Benedict, W. R. (2002). Perceptions of the police: Past findings, methodological issues, conceptual issues and policy implications. *Policing: an international journal of police strategies & management*.
https://web.archive.org/web/20120813064754id_/http://www.observatoriodeseguranca.org:80/files/p543.pdf

Culhane, S. E., Hosch, H. M., & Heck, C. (2008). Interrogation technique endorsement by current law enforcement, future law enforcement, and laypersons. *Police Quarterly, 11*(3), 366-386.
https://journals.sagepub.com/doi/abs/10.1177/1098611107309116

Dine, R. L. (2020). You shall bury him: burial, suicide and the development of Catholic law and theology. *Medical humanities*, *46*(3), 299-310. https://mh.bmj.com/content/46/3/299.abstract

English Standard Version. (2022). BibleGateway. https://www.biblegateway.com/passage/?search=John%2016:12-14&version=ESV (Original work published 2001).

Falcone, D. N., Wells, L. E., & Weisheit, R. A. (2002). The small-town police department. Policing: *An International Journal of Police Strategies & Management, 25(2), 371-384. doi:10.1108/13639510210429419*

Inbau, F., Reid, J., Buckley, J., & Jayne, B. (2013). *Criminal interrogation and confessions*. Jones & Bartlett Publishers. ISBN:13:978-0-7637-9936-6

Jackson, J., Bradford, B., Hough, M., Myhill, A., Quinton, P., & Tyler, T. R. (2012). Why do people comply with the law? Legitimacy and the influence of legal institutions. *British journal of criminology*, *52*(6), 1051-1071. https://eprints.bbk.ac.uk/id/eprint/5041/1/5041.pdf

Kelley v. Johnson, 425 U.S. 238 (1976)

Legitimacy Policing in Depth (n.d.). Rand Corporation. https://www.rand.org/pubs/tools/TL261/better-policing-toolkit/all-strategies/legitimacy-policing/in-depth.html

Leo, R. A., & Liu, B. (2009). What do potential jurors know about police interrogation techniques and false confessions?. *Behavioral Sciences & the Law*, *27*(3), 381-399. https://onlinelibrary.wiley.com/doi/abs/10.1002/bsl.872

McCormack, W. U. (1994). Grooming and weight standards for law enforcement: The Legal Issues. *FBI L. Enforcement Bull.*, *63*, 27. https://heinonline.org/HOL/LandingPage?handle=hein.journals/fbileb63&div=48&id=&page=

Midkiff, M. (2020). Professional Grooming Standards in 21st Century Policing. The Bill Blackwood Law Enforcement Management Institute of Texas. https://shsu-ir.tdl.org/handle/20.500.11875/3089

Murphy, K., Hinds, L., & Fleming, J. (2008). Encouraging public cooperation and support for police. *Policing & society*, *18*(2), 136-155. https://www.researchgate.net/profile/Jenny-Fleming/publication/249035231_Encouraging_Public_Cooperation_and_Support_for_Police/links/5b0e5136a6fdcc809959b81b/Encouraging-Public-Cooperation-and-Support-for-Police.pdf

New American Standard Bible. (2022). Bible Hub. https://biblehub.com/nasb/matthew/7.htm (Original work published 1995)

New King James Version. (2022). BibleGateway. https://www.biblegateway.com/passage/?search=Psalm%2082%3A3-4&version=NKJV (Original work published 1982)

Legitimacy Policing in Depth (n.d.). Rand Corporation. https://www.rand.org/pubs/tools/TL261/better-policing-toolkit/all-strategies/legitimacy-policing/in-depth.html

Ruffell, A., & McKinley, J. (2014). Forensic geomorphology. *Geomorphology, 206,* 14-22. https://www.sciencedirect.com/science/article/abs/pii/S0169555X13006284

Ruffell, A., & McKinley, J. (2005). Forensic geoscience: applications of geology, geomorphology and geophysics to criminal investigations. *Earth-Science Reviews, 69*(3-4), 235-247. https://pureadmin.qub.ac.uk/ws/files/372880/Ruff&McK_forensic.pdf

Schaffer, J. & Navarro, J. (2010). Advanced Interviewing Techniques: Proven Strategies for Law Enforcement, Military, and Security Personnel. Charles C. Thomas, ISBN978-0-398-07942

Taylor, S. (2019). *Forensic psychology: The basics.* Routledge. ISBN: 978-0-8153-7818

Timming, A. R., & Perrett, D. I. (2017). An experimental study of the effects of tattoo genre on perceived trustworthiness: Not all tattoos are created equal. *Journal of Trust Research, 7*(2), 115-128. https://www.tandfonline.com/doi/abs/10.1080/21515581.2017.1289847

Warren, J., Reboussin, R., Hazelwood, R. R., Cummings, A., Gibbs, N., & Trumbetta, S. (1998). Crime scene and distance correlates of serial rape. *Journal of Quantitative Criminology, 14*(1), 35-59. https://link.springer.com/article/10.1023/A:1023044408529

www.ingramcontent.com/pod-product-compliance
Lightning Source LLC
Chambersburg PA
CBHW060803260726
48660CB00002B/756